Out of the Blue

Poems and Stories

By

David Anthony

For Claudia, who saved me

Out of the Blue

The bolt of lightning crashed into the tree--
And stuck.
Leaves exploded into nuggets of popcorn,
Covering the ground.
 I awoke to find the blue-white shaft protruding from the tree
Like a fluorescent erection.
Wading through the knee-deep drifts of white,
I plugged my typewriter into the base of the tree
And typed "therefore" at the top of the page.

Black Bird

The soot-covered sparrow
Flew out from the fireplace
Leaving a wing print on the ceiling
Like a black rose painted on a tombstone--
And though I urged her toward the open window
She circled the room, returning
Again and again
To the nest which glowed in the ashes
And the featherless body we pulled from the fire.

Portside

First ice sculpts the shore,
November blows white
Over the widow's walks and high peaks
Of the wooden houses along the lake shore
Houses built when Marquette still looked toward Superior.
No footprints trample the drifts
Which lie against the iron grating.
No women wait, perched on rooftops
Looking over long distances
For the wooden ships to return.
Still, antique houses remain,
Tracing the water's edge
Visual echoes of the long-sunken ships
Preserved beneath the onset of another winter.

Mushroom Hunting

"... my pictures are after all almost a cry of anguish, although in the rustic sunflower they may symbolize gratitude."
Vincent Van Gogh

Mushrooms grow overnight,
How large depends on the moon.
A lover told me that
In the drowsy moments between love and dawn,
And I pictured the moon prying tiny caps from the soil
As it raked the tides across the oceans:
Night poppies turning their soft flesh toward the smaller light
As sunflowers turn toward the larger.
Mushrooms grow from yesterday's vegetation
Like early morning poems
Scratched out in darkness.
These mushroom poems may never hang
Like sunflowers on gallery walls,
But they clear the ground,
Nurturing fecundity,
In the darker hours.

Angles

There is a crooked man,
Who walks the streets of my hometown.
He moves in right angles
His gait and spine born in different dimensions.
I watched his movement on the sidewalk
Tacking like a ship in storm-tossed seas,
Saw three shopping mall debutantes cross the street
Shrieking and giggling to avoid him.
"Fuck you," he shouted at their straight backs, running away,
"Who do you think you are?"

Empty

It might have lain for centuries,
Tanned, mummified,
Preserved by the desert winds and dark cave walls--
If not for the insects,
Laying their eggs in the way of insects,
Seeking out the openings of flesh,
The eyes, nose, lips, anus,
The wounds on the temple and wrists
The spear-pierced abdomen.
Beginning the process of decay and reclaiming,
Returning to the earth its due.

fifteen

Our sexes were still hidden then,
Pestle and mortar grinding together
Our blue denim summer.
We burrowed into the couch in your parent's house,
Your nipples round and dark as Hershey's kisses.
Words like gasps of air from failed swimmers passed between us,
Promises or prayers made to the sex
Which pulled and twisted us into embraces.
You rocked your hips against me,
Whispered my name and I came,
Semen flowing into the folds of my jeans.
Later, I rode my bike home under streetlights,
Air blowing coldly against my skin.
I pedaled faster, turning my body,
Boy and man,
Into the wind.

Small Towers

The Crone and the Maiden--
Cycles of days.
Faces of men--
Winking, smiling.
Figures of animals--
Leaping, dancing.
Seas of purest water.

Still, easiest sight of all,
We see on the moon's surface
Exactly what we want to see.

But once, in Oregon moonlight
I plucked the moon from its elliptical vine
Closed my lips around moonflesh glowing.
My hands kneaded the moon
Forming small towers
Which we climbed, breathless
Gazing out over the luminous fields below.

Green Apples

After summer sunsets, we climbed to the elementary school roof
And threw green apples at the Chapins' house,
Crouching and running when the police searchlight
Pulled across the schoolyard like a bed sheet.

We watered furrows of corn,
Seeding the ground for night crawlers
Which we collected by flashlight
Holding their moist bodies tightly
As they stretched toward the earth.

We told our sisters about the haunted shacks
Where ghosts of railroad workers still dwelled,
Years after the fires trapped them in their beds.
And we laughed, elbowing each other
As they ran in to tell our mothers.

After summer sunsets, after our sisters were in the house asleep,
We tossed our comic books into one corner of the tent,
Shook the last of the electricity from our flashlights
And lay awake in sleeping bags,
Remembering the stories we had told
 And listening for the sound of burning footsteps.

Portia

Portia left her husband
To become a sword swallower
In a traveling circus.

        As part of her act
        She waved flaming batons through the air
        Trailing steel black smoke
        Pushed them slowly into her mouth
        Smothering the flames.

After the show
We met, made love
I smelled the thick kerosene
Tasted the acrid scars
Forming like children
In the darkness of her mouth.

Sultry

Even the air seems unfriendly
In an unfamiliar town
The heat finally dissipating into the companionship of dreams:
Lauren Bacall leaning against a door frame
With a glass in her hand,
Her body and gown cut from the same mold
Of black and white.
Curves covering her like steam rising from pavement
After an afternoon shower,
Carrying the scent of gin and perfume,
Damp grass and sweat,
Her hair falling on my face
Like a colorless rainbow.

The Hanged Man

Trees aren't supposed to look like this--
Painfully straight trunk, single limb crossing at a right angle--
And this is no saviour hanging from it,
Staring up from the card like an air-drowned fish,
Even though he wears a halo.
There are no nails or blood,
Only a reed twisted around one ankle suspends him,
Inverted from this rood. This is the trickster,
Smiling at the top-over world.
And this is not the Grouch Marx joke,
About not wanting to belong to any club
Who would have someone like me as a member.
This is the inverted poem, which came after a dream
About a boy standing alone on the edge of the playground,
Watching the other children play.
Children who, he imagined, did not lay awake at night
Listening to angry voices through the bedroom wall.
This is about the boy who dodged broken glass,
Who dreamed of moving in and out of games and conversations
Without leaving pieces of himself behind like bread crumbs.
This is not a poem about a person hanging upside down from a tree.
This is a poem about the teenager who swallowed shame in bottles on
the weekends,
And was force-fed shame in the public schools.
This is not a poem about a man, not a saviour,
Hanging upside down from a tree, a man with a halo.
This is a poem about a man
Hanging upside down
With the eyes of a child standing alone
On the edge of the playground.

Sanctuary/Sidewalk Pomegranate

She stood on the sidewalk,
Crying for a mother who was there
And then was not.
He knew how she felt,
A child, torn from her mother's hand,
Is in hell, a world of walking shadows.
He approached her cautiously
Took her hand, led her across the street
To the sterile darkness of the parking garage.
He wiped her tears, stroked her hair
Pulled her close to him
Until she was safe.

Poppies

The Red Cedar River crested when I was eight;
Fish played hopscotch in the flooded cemetery.

Your mother cut your red-poppy hair high off your shoulder;
We tied the strands into lures, and trolled the graves for trout.

The Indian Book said that pieces of your soul lived in your hair;
That cut hair was a gift from woman to man.

I released every fish we caught back into the blood-red current;
So that part of you would always live in the river.

That summer, everywhere you touched me,
Wine flowed from holes the size of your fingers;
And I drank cup after cup of your red hair.

BUS RIDE

I was standing at the bus stop with my coat draped over my arms. November had receded into September since I left home that morning, and people walked past me in shorts and sunglasses. Two college girls, their legs white after months out of the sun, looked at my coat, half-smiling. I wanted to stop them and explain that it had been a lot colder when I went to work. But I didn't.

When the bus came I climbed aboard and paid my dollar fare. The bus was always crowded at five o'clock and the only seats open were in the front of the bus, and reserved for handicapped and elderly persons. These seats were against the sides of the bus, facing the aisle. I sat down and decided I would move if someone came on who needed the seat.

The only other person sitting in the reserved seats was a woman of about thirty five. Her hair was uncombed. She wore an orange jacket, unbuttoned, and very old blue jeans. Her eyes stared unfocused out the window, her lips moving quickly and silently. She held on to the bar beside her seat with her right hand, and her fingers danced along the bar like she was playing the saxophone.

I looked away quickly and fought against watching her. There is something fascinating about those people who live on the edges of society. I avoid meeting them, but can't keep myself from staring when I do.

The woman laughed loudly to herself, two short barks. I looked up and she was staring at me. Her eyes seemed too large for her face. She stared with such intensity I blushed. I folded my coat neatly across my lap, brushed some dirt from my pants leg. When I looked up again she was staring out the window again.

The bus stopped and a black man got on. He wore a light red sweater and carried a black backpack. His eyes searched the crowded bus, then sat down across from me, beside the woman with the orange jacket. We rode for a few more blocks, stopping as people got on and off the bus. I was trying to catch his eye, to find some way of warning him, but nothing came to mind. Then the woman turned toward him. He was looking out the window and turned his head casually, smiling.

"How about some Pepsi?," the woman shouted. She waited a few seconds, like she expected him to respond, then began rocking back and forth.

The man's smile disappeared. His eyebrows pressed over his eyes and he looked at the woman. A smile passed quickly over his face and he started laughing.

The woman stopped rocking and turned toward him again. "That was a good one!," she said, as the man's laugh grew louder.

I turned sideways in my chair, to avoid seeing them and to stop the laugh I felt building within me. A woman sitting nearby glanced at me, shaking her head.

"Oh God," the man exhaled through his laughter. The woman was staring right at him, studying him. His expression would have been terrifying if he had not been laughing. He put his head back, trying to catch his breath, and I saw a gold filling flash from one of his rear teeth.

"I'm not the only one," the woman whispered. I couldn't stop myself any longer, and began to laugh too. The black man bent over with his head between his knees.

"I can't stop," he said, wiping his eyes. "How do I stop?"

Many people on the bus were laughing now. In the rearview mirror I saw the bus driver smiling. I looked down. It just didn't seem right, laughing at this poor, sick woman.

"That was a good one," she said again. Then she stopped laughing and stared out the window again. Her fingers played across the bar and she rocked slightly. Slowly everyone stopped laughing, except when the man would catch my eye, and we'd both look away to fight back a grin.

We both got up when the bus arrived downtown. "Bye," the woman said to us, smiling brightly. "Good luck."

"Goodbye," I said. The man got off in front of me and I stood on the sidewalk, watching his back as he walked away. The bus door closed behind me and a wave of heat and fumes swept by me as it pulled away. I threw my coat over my shoulder and walked the rest of the way home.

****

I got out of class late and had to run to catch my bus. I had been late to work twice this week and couldn't afford to be late again. The bus driver saw me running and waited for me to catch up. I was out of breath when I got on. I thanked the driver for waiting and showed her my pass. There were only a couple seats open near the front of the bus, so I sat down next to an older white woman.

I really hate riding the bus. There are so many weird people. The woman next to me kind of smelled, like she hadn't showered in a couple days. There was a white guy sitting across from me, who kept looking at me, then looking at the woman next to me. A bus full of whacko white people.

I could see this woman staring at me from the corner of my eye. I ignored her for a couple minutes, but she just kept staring. Then I saw the white guy across the aisle staring at me, too. God, I thought, they must be related.

I smiled at the woman, trying to be friendly. She stared at me with these big eyes and asked me if I wanted some Pepsi. Then she started laughing, a really nasty laugh, like she was choking. It sounded like when you try to start your car after it's already started. I tried not to laugh, but I couldn't help it. She had some really nasty breath, too.

"That was a good one," she said to the guy across the aisle. He started laughing. I lost it then. I put my head between my knees, laughing so hard I couldn't breathe. I tried to stop laughing, but every time I looked up one of those two was looking at me, and I would just lose it again.

"I'm not the only one," she whispered. Then she stopped laughing. I looked up, and she was sitting back, staring out the window. The guy was still smiling at me, with this stupid smile on his face. So I looked at the floor most of the way downtown.

When I got to my stop I stood up, and saw the guy following me. I didn't look at him. He and his friend said goodbye, and he got off after me. I could feel him watching me as I walked away, and I walked a little faster. When I turned around, he was still standing at the bus stop. I hate taking the bus.

****

1 2 3 4 5 1 2 3 4 5....

I sat on the hard plastic seat and stared out the window. Trees and houses flew by quickly. Faces stared out at me from the branches, geometric shapes alluding to metageometrical ideals danced along the eaves of blurred houses. My fingers counted time on the bar I grasped, dividing the passing scenery into five second increments, easier to integrate and identify.

The bus stopped and my counting became more focused. My eyes studied the framed reality of the bus window, looking in shrubs, through the outline of branches and lawns.

A figure passed before me, catching my attention. A man carried a brown coat. I stared at the intricate patterns of folds in the fabric, like a field of darkness flowing through skin.

12345 12345 12345 12...

3.4 secular increments. This was not the man. They would never send him on an uneven secular increment. I was sure of that. I studied his face. Short beard, light perspiration. No, it wasn't him.

The bus moved again. I stared out the window. The constant refrain of time played in my neurocardiointestinal system. 12345 12345. I searched the passing reality for any clue, any sign of irregularity.

The bus stopped. 12345 12345 12345 12345 12345 12345 123 The bus began again. A man sat beside me. I felt disappointed. I had thought this might be him. A white van passed by the window. P E P S I, I read off the side of the van.

12345 PEPSI 12345 PEPSI....

Of course! I realized at once the implication. A quick glance assured me I was right. The man across the aisle was staring at me, staring at the new man staring at me. Trying to tell me something.

12345 PEPSI 12345 PEPSI

A combination! Of course. They sent two messengers, to avoid any possible interception. With a flash of light, I realized their secular increments added together equaled a full secular component.

3.4 6.6 12345 PEPSI

I searched the man's outline. The dark hair, tight curls hiding like the dark folds of the other man's coat. The man seemed to read my thoughts, turned to me and smiled.

Yes, this is the one.

"How about some Pepsi?," I shouted. A rush of relief passed over me. Long years of waiting for the proper convergence, over at last.

A look of pain passed over the man's face. Across the aisle the other messenger stared at me, angrily. What had I done? Of course! How stupid! I had disclosed their purpose to all these strangers on the bus. Who knows how many of them were infiltrators, sent by the enemy to prevent the coming convergence.

Then the man began to laugh. Now both of them were laughing. I realized at once they were laughing to throw anyone who might have heard my comment off the track. A joke, of course a joke. If they were called before the Grand Tribunal, they would claim it had all been a joke.

"That was a good one," I said loudly, to assure anyone listening that I had only been joking. I laughed even louder.

"Oh God," the man beside me said and bent his head between his knees. I could tell he was as overcome as I was.

"I'm not the only one," I whispered. I wanted to let him know I had not been wasting my time. I had established a network of contacts, on both sides, ready to do whatever was necessary.

"Oh God, I can't stop," he said. "How do I stop?"

I knew he had been pressed too far too soon. I stopped laughing, suddenly worried that the fate of the convergence and the secular control I had worked for was now in the hands of one so weak. At least the other messenger seemed more in control.

I decided right away not to trust in these two. Despite their intentions, they did not seem equal to the task. It took a supreme will and constant devotion to ensure success.

I caught the rhythm of the secular increments again and watched out the window for any signs or portents of their future.

12345 12345 PEPSI 12345 12345 PEPSI

The bus stopped again, and the two messengers rose. The reality viewer showed a hopeful picture, a tall building with many dark windows, a pigeon walking on the thirteenth window ledge. I waited until the pigeon had flown and away, and I knew it was safe.

"Bye," I said daringly to the first messenger. "Good luck," I whispered.

"Goodbye," he said. The bus pulled out slowly.

12345 12345 12345 12345 .....

Yeti

These were the tools of his trade. Roger worked quietly in the shallow light emanating from the candle, packing his climbing gear into his blue nylon backpack. The stone walls of the hut obscured the wind but not the cold, and the thin mats covering the dirt floor did little more than cushion the impact of his boots on the earth. The sparse furnishings -- a mat covered with thick blankets where he had slept and a single table -- added no comfort. Although he had been in Tibet three weeks and had grown accustomed to the lifestyle of the people, his thoughts of home, and of Deborah, came no less frequently.

Before packing, Roger had taken careful inventory of each item. This was something he had learned on his first expedition with his father, when Roger was 17. "Up on a mountain, the only thing you've got is what you can carry. If it's at the base of the mountain or in Peoria, it don't matter. If it's not here, you don't have it." That had made sense to Roger at 17, and still did at 37. Since his father's death

Roger had become more aware of the things he had passed on to his son, things spoken and often unspoken. He hoped this trip would put to rest some of those memories.

Roger heard a low cough from outside the window and knew his sherpa was waiting for him. He finished packing, slipped on his parka and mittens, and slung the loaded pack over his shoulders. He looked around the room. Bare silence. The emptiness of this place wore heavier on him than any pack. Thinking of Deborah, he wondered whether this trip had been worth the cost. He blew out the candle and stepped through the doorway and into the pre-dawn shadows.

The guide sat on his cloth pack, leaning against the stone wall of the hut. He held the bowl of a pipe in one hand, its long curved stem clenched firmly between his teeth. His short, rocky stature and clothing of ochre and grey hand-spun fabric made him appear part of the landscape. His skin seemed to be dyed the same hue as the red cloth he wore. His high forehead and worn, rugged appearance made him blend into the stone wall. Roger looked down self-consciously at his brightly colored, manufactured clothing. He saw himself as he must appear to these people. He was tall and thin, with deep set eyes and a sharp nose and chin. Sharp, not rugged, he thought. He was no match for this climate. He had hoped that, by retracing the path his father had taken through the Himalayas forty years ago, he could form a bridge between himself and the memory of his father -- a bridge the two had never been able to build while he was alive.

The man stood as Roger approached. He was a gruff, taciturn man who Roger had met and hired his first day in-country. He spoke English well enough when he had the need, but for the most part was silent, except when scolding Roger for falling behind, or warning him of some danger ahead. Roger nodded a greeting and the man handed him the wooden pipe, which he accepted. Roger inhaled deeply and the bowl glowed red and hot.

The sun had not yet risen, but diluted colors were becoming visible. The hut was one of many which formed a semicircle facing toward the village center. Light snow dusted the ground. People had filled the emptiness the night before, and Roger knew his arrival had been met with a celebration whose aim was at once to welcome him and to move him on the next day. A few chickens and a goat milled about the kiva unattended, though Roger was aware of the smell of smoke and the sound of people stirring behind the thick walls. Roger pulled the straps of his pack tighter. He was ready to go.

The man took the pipe back from Roger and placed it back between his teeth. "You sleep good?" he asked in clipped but precise English.

"Yes. Thank you." Roger looked toward the east and the almost emerging sun, then toward the west where the day's journey would take them. "Are we ready to go?"

The guide blew smoke into the air, watching it disappear on invisible currents. "Storm tonight. Maybe today. We should stay here one more day."

Delay had haunted Roger since leaving Seattle. His only hope to work things out with Deborah was to do what he had to do and return. He did not want to waste even a single day.

"Is there another village along the way? We've only got a week's traveling left. I want to keep moving."

"No village for two days."

"We can take shelter somewhere if the storm hits, can't we? We've ridden out enough weather already. One more blast can't be that bad."

Roger spoke confidently, but the memory of that first storm was with him still. Nothing had prepared him for those winds that had swept through every layer of his clothing, as he huddled beneath the granite shelf that the sherpa had called shelter. He had survived though. He knew that survival was a reward, and the only lasting motivation in the mountains.

"Maybe." The guide drew on the pipe again then tapped the bowl against the palm of his hand, scattering the glowing contents on the ground. Roger watched them glowing in the darkness, reminding him of tea leaves spread out on a fortune teller's table.

"There is a temple. Get there today, maybe. No one stays there."

"A temple, great." Roger spoke without enthusiasm. "We'll head for the temple. If the storm hits, we can stay there and ride it out."

Muttering in his own language, the guide shook his head. "No. No one stays there."

"Well then, no one will mind if we do. What do you say we get moving? It's light already."

The guide tossed his pipe into his cloth pack, still muttering. From the tone of his voice, Roger thought he might be cursing. His roughhewn hands removed a small bundle from his pack. It was wrapped in animal skin and fastened to a hide strap. He placed it around his head like a necklace. Holding the bundle in his left hand, he closed his eyes and spoke to himself, slowly and deliberately.

Roger could not understand the words but found the ceremony unsettling. He shoved his hands into the pockets of his parka and scanned the horizon, searching for signs of the storm the guide had spoken of. He could see nothing which presaged the future. The guide grew silent. Without any warning, he set off down the path and out of the village. Roger followed him.

They moved away from the glowing light of morning which had caused the snow and stones to take on a reddish glow. The effect faded rapidly and soon the trail before them was illuminated. Roger fell quickly into the walking rhythm he had followed for the past week, his eyes following the strong back before him, matching the guide's stride. He concentrated on the increasing light, the sparse vegetation and the gravely path that shifted and scraped with every step. The monotony of the journey had overtaken him within a few days. His father had talked with excitement of his years in Tibet and China, and for most of his life Roger was in awe of the experience, wondering what he had missed in his suburban lifestyle. During his youth, he had accompanied his father on three climbs, two in Northern Canada and one in Alaska. It was while he and his father were on the expedition to Mt. Alymer that Roger's mother had been killed in the accident. They arrived ten days after the funeral.

The coldness of his father's reaction had affected Roger. Even when they visited the grave his father had not cried, and within a week he had begun planning another expedition, this time to South America. Roger was 17, and decided then he would never travel with his father again. Roger needed his father to tell him it was all right to mourn, but sadness was something his father could not allow in himself, and did not acknowledge in his son. Roger had survived. He had gone off to college and the distance between he and his father grew beyond numbered miles. By they time he and Deborah were married, Roger's father had become an outsider, and for ten years he had remained a stranger, on the fringes of Roger's life and thoughts.

Until his stroke. For the few months that his father had lived, first in the hospital then in the nursing home, the stranger on the fringe of Roger's thoughts had become a screaming figure of urgency. His father never spoke after the stroke, and only rarely did Roger's visits even spark a look of recognition. After his father finally passed, Roger seemed to be mourning not for his father, or even his long-dead mother. Roger seemed to be mourning a life wasted. Deborah's attempts to console him did not comfort him. He seemed to feel a rage building, not directed at Deborah or himself. It was a shout from within him, and it was directed at that man who still circled his life like a silent, lifeless rock floating in outer space. Deborah had tried to understand, but when he announced he was quitting his job and traveling to Tibet, she had left.

Deborah. Her name became a refrain on his long marches, a valley where all his thoughts flowed like mountain streams. He wondered if she would be waiting for him when he returned. Could she let the last year drop away, fading like an illness that had forced them apart for a time? Could he return to the life of alarm clocks, mortgage payments and sharing his life?

Without really seeing his surroundings, Roger stared at the back of the man in front of him, the deepening snow to the right and left of the trail and the incline of the path beneath his feet. Prolonged walking is a meditation, he thought. What enters our minds in that time of unconscious action is what drives our lives. Buddhists, he knew, thought to silence that voice, the self, that filled the silence. Roger thought, almost smiling, that had learned the truth of his western mind. He wanted to hear the thoughts that guided him, not to silence them, but to own them. He needed to control them, rather than letting them control him. Would that insight survive when he stopped walking, he wondered. Or when he landed at the Sea-Tac Airport?

Deborah would not share this insight. She always lived in her life as a swimmer in the sea. There was no division between her self, her body and her life. At least he had never been aware of any division. A swimmer, he thought, does not know the impact of legs striking earth. Swimmers propel themselves through the element of their motion, and that element opens and closes behind them. Walkers move through the air, but must strike the ground to drive themselves. There is a unity in the motion of swimmers, and conflict in the motion of walkers.

Roger shook himself from this reverie. Why couldn't Deborah understand why he needed to do this? He looked at his surroundings again -- the grey stone cliffs and the blowing wind which Roger realized was now gusting menacingly -- and knew that this distance had always been there, between them, invisible. She could not see that part of him, the part that was his father. But it had always been there, pulling Roger away from his life and toward this place.

The sun was high now, though it offered little warmth. Through the morning, his shadow had stretched forward, but now it retracted, barely covering the ground beneath him. The sky to the west had thickened with clouds, and a strong wind was beginning to place itself in their path. When the guide squatted down near the trail, Roger was relieved and dropped his pack from his shoulders. They throbbed when the weight was removed and Roger sat on a stone rubbing his upper arms through the heavy parka. The guide knelt in the snow with his head bowed, examining the trail. He looked up and stared at the gathering clouds. Roger opened his pack, taking out a bag of chocolate he had carried with him. He rationed out three squares and put them in his mouth, letting them warm and melt.

The guide stood up quickly and his hand grasped the bundle around his neck. He looked in all directions, as if afraid he might find what he was looking for.

"Yeti," he said hoarsely.

"What? What is it?"

The man looked back to Roger. "Yeti," he said again, making a deep growling sound in his throat. "Wait," he shouted over his shoulder, dashing off to the left of the trail.

"Hey!" Roger shouted, as he watched his guide disappear around a bend in the cliff wall. Roger watched for a moment for the figure to reappear. Sighing heavily, he rose. He stepped off the path and examined the spot where the man had been crouching. There were tracks in the snow, large tracks. They headed off in the same direction the guide had taken. They were hard to see, but looked almost human. Roger could make out the impression of a heel, and what seemed like toes. Who would be barefoot up in these mountains?," he wondered. Maybe someone had gotten lost. That was why his guide had run off, to try and find them. Or some monk. He had heard that there were Buddhist monks in the area who lived like hermits.

Roger remembered the temple his guide had mentioned and assumed it must be nearby. Thank God, Roger said to himself, with a glance at the darkening sky. Yeti, he thought. Perfect. With a storm approaching, his guide was off chasing the abominable snowman. He sat down again and waited, watching the turn in the cliff face for a figure to return. The winds had strengthened and the clouds were moving in quickly. He should have listened. Deborah had pleaded with him not to go. This whole trip had seemed crucial, but now he wondered what he had been expecting. His father had told exciting stories of being the first white man to visit some of the villages he encountered. There were feasts and the giving of gifts. He had even been offered the daughter of a village elder as a wife. The people Roger met had learned not to be astonished at the color of his skin. There was no mystery or wonder in their reactions to them, or his to them. Roger had come to Tibet to find the unknown, but he realized there were no blank spots on the map any longer. There was nothing for him to find, except himself.

The guide had been gone too long, and Roger was annoyed. Single flakes of snow had begun to blow in the wind and the temperature was dropping. He put the bag of chocolate into the pocket of his parka. Cursing under his breath, he left his pack behind and followed the footsteps into the drifts of snow.

The going was not easy. As soon as he left the trail the snow became knee deep. Before he got to the spot where the guide had vanished, the snow was even higher. He wondered how anyone could have moved so quickly to through the white field. The drifts lessened where the cliffs blocked the wind, but the trail itself became less clear. There seemed to be several paths. He could not see which, if any, had been made by his guide. He shouted a few times into the swirling silence. Nothing.

He did not want to go forward, for fear of losing the trail or missing the guide when he returned. But the sky was dark now, and flakes bigger than his thumb were falling steadily. He had decided to return to the trail when he saw a dark opening in the rock face, about 100 feet away. As he approached, he could see it was a large cave. The opening was almost as tall as he was. The wind blew across the mouth of the cave and it seemed to moan. The lonely sound grew louder as he drew nearer. The entrance had regular borders and seemed man-made, as if it had been cut out of the 40 foot high cliff wall by hand.

Placing one arm against the cliff, Roger peered inside. No light extended past the entrance. He heard the sounds of the wind playing against the stone walls, and it seemed for a moment the cave was inhaling and exhaling, breathing in light and breathing out darkness.

"Hello," he shouted. His voice echoed and returned, hollow and unrecognizable. Roger looked for any sign of the guide. He looked at the sky. Snow fell thickly on his face. Even the dark clouds were lost now in a rising flurry. There seemed no choice. He would wait out the storm here.

He headed back, following the edge of the cliff back toward the trail where he had left his pack. After only a few steps, he knew that it was hopeless. The snow had drifted even higher, rising almost to his chest. He could barely make out the spot where he had last seen the guide. He could no longer see the trail. His pack seemed to have vanished completely. The snow had drifted over every trace. He could not risk getting lost in the storm. He turned back to the cave.

The mouth of the cave was set back into the rock and was sheltered somewhat from the snow. Roger sat down on a patch of bare ground and watched the snow accumulate. There seemed nothing else to do. He cursed himself for leaving his pack behind. His father's words came back to him but he shut them out. They were no help. Emptying his pockets, he examined their contents. Besides his bag of chocolate, he had a butane lighter, a pack of cigarettes, and a waterproof packet which held his passport, birth certificate, a photograph of Deborah and two letters he had written her during his travels.

He broke off another piece of the chocolate. Eight squares left. The storm could last hours, maybe days. He would have to make them last. And he would have to keep the mouth of this cave from drifting over. If that happened, he might never get out. He put the papers and chocolate back into his pocket. The wind seemed to have lessened, and the howling had quieted. Holding the lighter above his head, Roger moved into the recesses of the cave. The small flame sent flickering shadows across the wall. Each movement of his hand made the walls seem to come alive with motion. He put his left shoulder against the rock and slowly stepped a few paces back into the darkness. His feet shuffled across small stones on the cave floor. The stone wall jutted out in places and he moved slowly to avoid striking his legs or arms.

Something brushed against his leg and he stepped back quickly. Holding the lighter lower, he saw a pile of stick and some larger pieces of wood placed in a pile. What the hell?, he thought. But he didn't waste time wondering. He gathered the wood together. Breaking up the smaller sticks, he made a small pyramid and held his lighter beneath it. The metal grew hot and he switched hands often as the sticks smoked. After a moment, a small flame started. He added larger sticks until the fire caught fully.

Deborah would be proud, he thought. Whenever they went camping she tended the fire, saying he couldn't burn his way out of a paper bag with a flame-thrower. No. He knew Deborah would not be proud. She would be angry, scared, livid: anything but proud. Reaching into his pocket took out her picture and studied it in the firelight. The flickering shadows seemed to add years to her face, then take them away again. Roger noticed that the photo, his hand, even the walls of the cave seemed to leap and transform in the light, as if nothing were quite solid or real.

The howling wind changed pitch and a burst of snow swept into the cave, littering the floor and gutting the flame as if it were a candle. Roger stood at the entrance and looked out. A total whiteout. The storm showed no signs of letting up. Staring into the white, Roger thought he could make out movement a few yards away. He shouted once, then convinced himself it was a trick of the storm. He sat down beside the fire.

His father had told him once, "There's no room for a woman on a mountain. The air's too cold and too thin." Now he understood what his father had meant. As much as he missed Deborah, he was glad she was not there, sharing the danger with him. She would probably handle it better than he, though. She was much more practical, and a better grasp on life. He did wish he were with her right now, sitting across from her at the dinner table, or guiding their car through traffic in downtown Seattle.

He remembered the letters he had written her and took them out. How much he loved her. How much he wanted her to understand. How much crap. He wanted her to justify him, nothing more. He was alone in the storm, cut off with no food and no help. He could die in this cave, in this cold world he had accepted as a birthright from his father, that he had taken in exchange for his own life. That had been his decision. It had been a wrong decision. But he would accept the consequences. He knew the truth of those consequences, but he still had a need for her to say that it was OK, that he had made a good choice, though not the right choice.

There was no room for such deceit in this cave, it could find no purchase in this wind. She could not justify him, the memory of her could not save him from this. He knew there was a part of him that he did not, could not love -- part of him that was his father. He had learned that, if nothing else, on this journey. Unless he learned to love that part of himself, he could never let Deborah love him, as much as she might want to. Tearing up the two letters, he tossed them into the fire. They added little warmth or light.

Deborah.

Roger heard his father's voice again, suddenly. "Alone in the mountains is bad enough. Alone, with a woman's name attached to it, is good for nothing but a gun in the mouth." He knew that this cave had been waiting for him all his life. This was part of him too, these cold stone walls. He could not deny them. But they were not all of him. They could not define him, unless he let them.

Roger lay on the ground, almost expecting to cry. But only sleep came. A restless sleep that seemed almost as threatening as the storm outside the cave. Roger dreamed of his home. He was shouting for Deborah, but she was not there. The house was empty. All the furniture was gone, the lamps and lights. A huge fire filled the center of the living room, burning without any fuel. The walls of the house turned into grey stone and the ceiling was a dark cloud, which swirled like a hurricane's eye above the fire. Blowing snow drifted in the corners. A man appeared out of the storm, Roger's father, wearing the guide's clothes. He held in one hand the cloth bundle the guide had worn around his neck. With his other hand he pointed to the far corner of the room. From beneath the drift he saw a piece of cloth exposed. He knelt and dug frantically, tugging at the frozen arms and legs. Pulling Deborah's blue face and lips toward him, he kissed her and waited for the snow to cover them both.

He awoke with a gasp. The wind had changed again, and snow blew over his face. Somewhere, beneath the howling, Roger heard a sound like breathing. Roger pulled away, seeking the surety of the stone walls, seeking to put the fire between himself and the storm. Snow and wind washed into the cave, almost extinguishing the fire. Dark shapes swept all around him, shapes that grew in intensity with the breathing sounds. Roger knelt, feeling as if the cave itself were lowering upon him.

Cold swept over him. With a gust of the storm, the sticks scattered and the fire was extinguished. Darkness. Roger pawed through the sticks, looking for a branch or an ember to use as a torch. Roger looked up as a shape approached from outside, silouhetted against the whiteout. The growling grew louder and Roger's own voice joined it, howling in protest. It was almost on him. The shape was becoming clearer, taking human form, but it seemed much larger than human.

Roger crouched, knowing that soon escape would be impossible. Remember who you are, he thought. You are your father's son. You are Deborah's husband. He sought frantically for a stick or stone, anything to use as a weapon. He put his hand in his pocket, pulled out something smooth and thin. He held it up close, and could just make out a face. He knew it was Deborah's face, but in the darkness he could not tell. It might be her face, or his, or even his father's. They ran together in the storm. Roger slipped it back into his pocket. The figure approached. Roger stood on the balls of his feet, his fists clenched. In the whiteness, he saw the red-ochre robes blowing in the wind.

The Endurance of Wood

JoAnn's uncle had lived alone for years, ever since his wife died. Much of the house had been unused since then. In one room, eight years of newspapers had been tossed in, most of them unread and still in rubber bands. It was the house her mother grew up in, but JoAnn had never seen it. Now she and her husband, Richard, were looking over the letter from the Probate Attorney, deciding what their next step would be.

The attorney, Herb Lawrence, had sent her a picture of the house, along with a letter explaining that her Uncle Jonah had left specific instructions that she receive the building and all its contents. He went on to warn them of the house's condition. The plumbing leaked, the furnace was a fire hazard and needed replacing, and the roof would have to be reshingled. He offered to handle the sale of the house for them, if they decided not to keep it. JoAnn read the letter once, then twice, before handing it to Richard. She studied the photograph for a moment, frowning slightly, then placed it back inside the envelope.

"What do you think?," she asked. JoAnn watched Richard set the letter on the coffee table and sit back on the couch. Life with a lawyer, she thought. You never get a simple answer.

"Well, whatever you want to do is all right with me," he said. "But this Lawrence has probably got the right idea, as far as dollars and cents go."

JoAnn slipped off her shoes and sat beside him on the couch. She pulled the bangs of her red hair away from her forehead, then pushed them back into place.

"I never even knew my uncle," she said. "I can't imagine why he left me his house."

"Probate would probably have passed it to you anyway, if he hadn't named someone else."

JoAnn looked uncertainly to Richard. "And it's so far away. I can't ever see us living there, or even driving two hours to stay for vacations."

Richard pursed his lips and nodded his head noncommittally. "You're probably right. But you were his last living relative. And, it was your mother's home, too."

"A long time ago," she said. She reclined on the couch, stretching her feet out on the coffee table. "She only visited there once after I was born. Do you think I should have gone to his funeral?"

Richard laid his hand on JoAnn's knee and rubbed it gently. "None of them came to your mother's funeral. I wish you'd stop beating yourself up like this. There was no reason for you to go. You'd never met the man. You wouldn't have known anyone there. You weren't the one who broke the ties with your family. They made that choice long before you were born."

"I know. But I was his niece. I felt so bad when Mother died and no one from her family came. I can't stand to think of him dying and having no one there. I'd hate to ever be like that."

"You'll never be alone," Richard said. He pulled JoAnn's feet off the coffee table and put them in his lap. "You'll always have me, and Tobias and Alanna, and pretty soon there'll be grandchildren."

JoAnn smiled.

"He was alone because he chose to be alone," Richard continued and JoAnn heard his voice rise slightly, anger growing in his face. "They never cared when your mother moved to Detroit, and they didn't take any interest in you while you were growing up. All because your mother married a black man. Well, look at me! I'm as black as your father. Do you think they would have treated us any differently?"

JoAnn laughed. Watching Richard grow angry reminded her of her father. When she was young and misbehaved, he would scold her and become so angry that he couldn't speak. "I can't believe you would do this," he would say. "I mean the idea of it just makes me--" then he would put his hand to his forehead and walk away, mumbling.

"What's funny?" Richard asked, surprised by her laughter.

"The idea of it," JoAnn said, laughing again at his puzzled expression. "You should have taken up criminal law. I'd feel sorry for anyone facing you on the stand."

"I'd feel sorry for them too." He relaxed and touched JoAnn's shoulder lightly. "You uncle died alone because of his own bitterness. You weren't responsible for that.

"Jo, why do we have to make a decision on the house right away? In fact, why don't we take a drive up north some weekend and take a look at the house for ourselves? You probably shouldn't make a decision until you've at least seen the house for yourself."

"That's a pretty good idea," JoAnn said.

Bending down, he softly kissed JoAnn's ankles. "I have lots of good ideas."

JoAnn had taken the picture of the house with them and she looked at it as they drove north on I-75. It was a two story plank board farm house and had been painted light blue many years before. A maple tree cast a shadow over the tall peaked roof and large wooden window frames. She tried to imagine the house as it must have looked fifty years ago, when her mother was a child.

"Mother used to talk about that house all the time," she said to Richard. She rolled down the window, letting the spring warmth fill the car. "I used to wish I had grown up there. She talked a lot about her brother, and their friends. She told me there was a creek that ran about a mile behind their house, and on Friday nights she and her brother would catch worms and put them in an old Mason jar. Then Saturday morning they would wake up early and walk down to the creek and fish until lunchtime."

"You hate fishing," Richard said, looking at her from the corner of his eye.

JoAnn slapped him playfully on the arm. "That's not the point. She seemed to be filled with that house, even years after she left it. It gave her a sense of place. She lived there all her life, until the war started and she got a job in Detroit at the factory."

"Is that where she met your father?'

JoAnn nodded. She put one hand out the car window and let it dangle in the wind. "Yeah. They got married and then had me. As far as I know, she only went back once after that, just after I was born. She wanted her parents to see their grand daughter. She drove up with a friend from work, and my grandfather wouldn't even look at me. He went up to his room and wouldn't come out until we had gone."

JoAnn's mother had told her that story a few years before she died. She couldn't remember her mother ever looking so sad. She must have been sick even then, though if she knew it she didn't say anything. Her white hair had been pulled back and tied behind her head, and when she spoke JoAnn thought she looked older than she had ever looked before.

"When I talked to Herb Lawrence this morning, he said the house had been cleaned," Richard said. "They didn't throw anything away. They just cleaned and organized everything."

"Mother said that her home was always spotless. My grandmother was a firm disciple of the Cleanliness School. My mother was the same way. I guess I'm just a lazy fop."

"This is our exit," Richard said. JoAnn took out the letter again, and read the map the Probate lawyer had provided, directing her husband as he drove through the small downtown and past the tidy sidewalks and the few cars parked in front of the Ace Hardware and the drug store.

They turned off Main onto Sycamore and drove through the residential area. The houses were old, but mostly well-cared for. There were trees in every yard; trees older than the house she and Richard lived in. Some of the front yards were larger than the parks she had played in as a child. In one yard, two boys pushed a small girl in a tire swing; in another, a group of young men stood beside a car in a driveway. One boy lifted the hood of the car and their faces and heads disappeared from view.

"I wonder what it would have been like to have lived here," JoAnn said. "Everything seems so different than Detroit."

It was different too, JoAnn realized, from their home in Grosse Pointe. There was an authenticity here, in the way children drove their bikes across yards and left them leaned against front porches, in the old cars parked beside garages with grass grown tall around their wheels.

Driving slowly, Richard checked the speedometer and watched closely for children who were playing and riding bikes. JoAnn scanned the numbers on the passing mailboxes.

"This should be it right here," she said.

Richard pulled slowly into the gravel driveway. The house looked just like the picture, except the lawn had been mown and the bushes in front of the house were carefully trimmed. He parked the car and they both got out. Stretching his legs, he walked around the car to stand beside JoAnn.

"The utilities should be on," he said. He took JoAnn's hand and together they walked toward the house. JoAnn thought the house seemed to lengthen and grow as they approached. She began silently counting her steps, something she had learned to do as a child whenever she felt nervous. "Thirteen, fourteen, fifteen." JoAnn stepped onto the front porch and leaned down to retrieve the key from beneath the mat. She opened the door and stood for a moment, looking in."

"After you," Richard said, bowing slightly. JoAnn sighed and stepped through the doorway. She blinked a few times as her eyes adjusted to the dim interior light. The walls were a tainted off-white color, badly in need of scrubbing and new paint. Near the ceiling joint the paint had flaked off exposing the older, even greyer paint. The light from the open doorway echoed off the wood floor and illuminated the staircase opposite the door, which led to the second floor. JoAnn glanced quickly at the living room to her right and the kitchen to her let. The curtains in the living room were drawn, and the room had the dark tone of a forest at sunset. The kitchen was brighter, more friendly.

JoAnn sensed Richard standing beside her, waiting for her to take the lead. "Johnboy, Mary Ellen, we're home," JoAnn called into the house. The house swallowed the sound. Not very funny, she thought.

Richard smiled and stepped past her into the living room. He flicked a switch around the corner from the door and light from a large, ornate ceiling fixture filled the room. JoAnn followed him into a room filled with the bric-a-brac which JoAnn had expected to find in an old farmhouse -- souvenirs of county fairs, a photograph of a soldier standing below the Eiffel Tower, ceramic figurines of small animals and children. The television, a 1960s walnut-colored box standing on four thin legs, was placed at an awkward angle in one corner, beside the brick fireplace. Real brick, JoAnn thought. The hardwood floor was worn with the footsteps of eighty years, but had recently been polished and shone through with the endurance of wood.

JoAnn tried to imagine the people who lived in this house. It seemed so large for just one man and she knew her uncle must have been very lonely, living there since his wife had died. The furniture -- an old sofa covered with a green and white afghan pushed against the wall opposite the television, a wooden rocker with orange cushions next to the doorway, and a brown imitation leather recliner beside the fireplace -- seemed not to have been arranged, but to have placed for display on someone's front yard for a rummage sale.

Richard sat heavily in the recliner, and JoAnn laughed at his expression as the chair seemed to sigh and envelop him.

"And Goldilocks said 'this chair is too soft,'" he said.

JoAnn noticed that one wall was covered in photographs. From their appearance, the photos seemed to span a century of her family history. She looked into the faces for any resemblance to her mother or herself, for any sign of relationship between herself and these people. She recognized the picture of her grandfather standing in his World War One uniform; her mother had one just like it. Pictures of a bride and groom on their wedding day were in twin metal frames, facing each other. This must be her aunt and uncle. There was a picture of her red-haired grandmother posing stiffly in a flowered dress, her face turned at a slight angle. There were no pictures of her mother.

"You look a lot like your grandmother," Richard said.

"My mother used to tell me that."

JoAnn smiled and walked through the entryway and into the kitchen. She turned on the globe light which hung over the large oak table in the center of the room. The floor was yellow linoleum, the walls papered with faded yellow roosters and farmyard scenes. The cupboards were painted white.

She opened the cupboard closest to her. The shelves were covered with cracked and torn contact paper. The lower shelf had a stack of worn dinner plates and a mixed assortment of cups and saucers. JoAnn pulled a metal from chair away from the table and stood on it. From the higher shelf she took a crystal water glass, which caught the light from the ceiling and brimmed over with it. The crystal scattered the light, cascading rainbows over her hands. She turned to call for Richard and saw him standing in the doorway, watching her.

"This is beautiful," she said. Richard nodded.

"I don't know what to think," she said. "I can't convince myself that I own all this. Most of it is so, ugly I guess." She stepped down from the chair. "I feel like I'm rummaging through someone else's house."

She closed the cupboard door and slid the chair back to its place at the table. Richard walked to the window above the double sink, opened the curtains and pushed up the window. JoAnn could hear the sound of a motorbike whining somewhere not far away , and closer, a dog barking.

Turning on the faucet, Richard stepped back slightly as brownish-orange water ran out. He let the water run till it was clear, then turned the faucet off and closed the window.

"That was a good drive," he said. "Do you want to go find someplace to eat? We could look around the house some more later."

JoAnn shook her head. Somehow, she had begun to feel that her uncle had left her this house for a reason. It was irrational, but she felt there was something here she was supposed to find. She also knew that once she left this house, she would never return.

"No. Let's finish here first. We've got a long drive back, though."

JoAnn turned and left the kitchen, standing for a moment at the base of the staircase. She put her hand on the wood hand rail. Her footsteps sounded loudly on the risers as she climbed. She liked the feel of the railing in her hand, its coolness beneath her palm. It felt comfortable to her, in a way the rest of the house did not.

At the top of the stair was a hallway with two doors on either side. There was also a door at the end of the hall which was slightly ajar. JoAnn saw the white porcelain bathroom fixtures through the opening. On the hallway floor a runner carpet absorbed the sound of their footsteps on the wood.

More pictures hung in the hallway, older than those downstairs. A wooden oval frame hung on the right wall, and the glass expanded out from it in a thick hemisphere. Behind the glass was a photo of a young man in a Union Army uniform, holding an American flag. The picture hung at eye level, and Richard looked at it curiously as JoAnn opened the first door on the right.

The room was very dark. A thick curtain covered the window. She could see the silhouettes of boxes and furniture. She pulled back quickly as she saw the outline of a sewing dummy in the far corner. An uneasiness passed over her. From the doorway she looked over the boxes and as she opened the door wider light passed through the bars of a baby crib, casting a web-like shadow against the wall. She felt an urge to run. Maybe she should leave now. Maybe she did not want to find whatever her uncle had left for her.

Richard peered over her should into the room. "I doubt there are any antiques here," he said, "but we ought to have everything inventoried and appraised just in case. Who knows, we might make an appearance on Antiques Roadshow."

She could see that he was enjoying exploring the house much more than she was, and was surprised to find she resented it. This is my history, she thought, my family. It's not some circus sideshow or flea market. She wanted to tell him how she felt, but she knew it was unfair and wouldn't make any sense to him. She wasn't sure it made sense to her.

JoAnn turned away, and opened the door across the hall. This room was completely empty. She stepped in and looked around at the bare walls. The vacant space seemed to swirl sound like an ocean shell and JoAnn felt slightly dizzy. As she turned to go, she noticed something on the wall behind the open door. She closed the door partially and saw a photograph of two small children standing beside a large tree in front of the house. Her uncle wore a cowboy hat with a drawstring down around his chin, a toy gun and holster strapped to his waist. Beside him, a few inches short, was her mother. She had a short tomboyish haircut and wore a wrinkled dress with a bow in her hair. They were both smiling.

She wanted to stay with this photo for a moment, imagining the closeness of a brother and sister growing up -- a closeness she had never known as an only child. Her mother had loved her family. She knew that. That was why it had hurt so much. JoAnn pitied these people for their ignorance, and hated them for their betrayal of her and her mother. But she wanted to love them too, as her mother had. She thought her mother would want her to.

Richard had stayed out of the room, perhaps thinking JoAnn wanted some space, and opened the third door himself. When JoAnn stepped back into the hall, she saw him standing with an almost sad expression on his face, looking into the room. As JoAnn approached he stepped into the room, making room for her to follow. She saw him standing in a room with only a few feet of empty floor space. Newspapers were stacked all around the room. Piles of newspapers, many still folded and bound with rubber bands, were stacked on an old four-poster bed, on the floor beside the bed, piled high against every wall, and the papers completely covered an old, discolored walnut dresser.

For the first time, JoAnn really felt the presence of her uncle. She imagined him living her for eight years after his wife died. Every morning he took the newspaper from the doorstep, carried it up the stairs and threw it into this room, without even looking at it. She wondered if the newspaper were his only contact with the outside world. Maybe he didn't know how to read, she thought. Maybe he just kept getting the paper out of habit. Maybe the paper reminded him of something. Something he didn't want to forget.

"I should have gone to his funeral," she said. "He shouldn't have died all alone." This could be me, she thought. I could have been him.

She was crying softly and Richard pulled her close to him and put his arms around her. "It was not your fault," he said.

JoAnn nodded silently into his chest. She liked the smell of him, the feel of his chest through the thin shirt he wore. "When I was young I spent so much time alone," she said. "I never fit anywhere. I never felt I belonged anywhere."

"You belong with me," Richard said, stroking her hair.

"I know," she said, still crying. "But sometimes I don't feel that way. Sometimes I feel like I'm living in your house, like I raised your children. I hate feeling that way."

"Do I make you feel that way?" he asked, concerned.

"No. No, of course not." She pulled away from him and brushed her hair back into place. "I guess it's just because we moved so much when I was little. I never really felt at home anywhere."

"I love you," Richard said.

JoAnn smiled at him and stepped into the small bathroom at the end of the hall. She wiped her eyes and stood before the mirror.

"Look at me," she said.

"I am."

JoAnn turned to Richard, looking into his eyes. There's nothing in this house that belongs to me, she thought. There's nothing from this house I need.

He seemed to guess her thoughts. "There's one room left," he said.

JoAnn nodded. Walking past him she opened the final door. There was nothing on the walls. The only furnishings were a twin bed, a sable-colored dresser against one wall and a large wooden trunk at the foot of the bed. A patchwork quilt was folded over the lid of the trunk. The bed was neatly made and covered with a checkered bedspread. On the dresser were a picture of her aunt, and a small wooden box. JoAnn opened the box. Inside were two pairs of wire-rimmed reading glasses.

Richard took the quilt of the cedar trunk and laid it carefully on the bed. JoAnn knelt beside the trunk and opened the lid. She carefully lifted a white wedding dress from the trunk. The white lace seemed to dance in JoAnn's palm. She stood up and held the dress up to her. The odor of the cedar had permeated the fabric and JoAnn wanted to drink the smell in. It comforted her and reminded her of the potpourri she like to brew in her own kitchen.

Beneath the dress, a large book had been placed in the center of the trunk. Richard reached in and pulled it out, closed the trunk and placed the book on its lid. JoAnn lay the dress on the bed and knelt again, running her fingers over the book's cover. It had the texture of an elm tree; deep, rough furrows cut by time.

"A family Bible," Richard said quietly. "Now there's something you don't see every day."

JoAnn turned the cover over and touched the fragile thin pages. She ran her finger over the ornate type, the faded colors of gold and red. Pressed between the pages were newspaper clippings, old photographs. An envelope was placed somewhere in the book of Exodus. Inside the envelope, JoAnn found a black and white photograph of her mother. She stood on the porch outside the house. She was about twelve years old and her long hair hung over her shoulder. She wore a bright dress which was rumpled by the breeze.

Turning to the center of the book, JoAnn saw a series of names written in a precise hand. As she read each name, she placed it with the pictures she had seen throughout the house. Jonah Brimerton, born 1837, died Gettysburg, July 1863; Sarah Macomb (Brimerton), born 1841, died 1900. JoAnn studied the pages religously, noting the differences in handwriting, the ages of her family pressed between the pages in blue and black ink.

She saw her grandmother and her grandfather listed in turn. Her uncle's and her mother's name were written near the bottom of the page. Beside her uncle's name was written: Elaine Cofey (Brimerton) born April 1934, died November 27, 1998. There was no name written beside her mother's name.

JoAnn turned the page slowly. She read the words written in a trembling hand, the hand of an old man: JoAnn Freeman, born by the grace of God January 29, 1963. This is what he wanted me to find, she thought. This is why he left me the house. He wanted me to find this. He wanted to give me this.

JoAnn closed the Bible and Richard took her hand, helping her as she stood. She picked up the book and held it tightly in her hand, still holding Richard's with the other. She was ready to go home.